THE HOME
FRONT

THE HOME FRONT

ANN KRAMER

FRANKLIN WATTS
LONDON • SYDNEY

Franklin Watts
This edition published in Great Britain in 2015
by The Watts Publishing Group

Designer Jason Billin
Editor Constance Novis
Art Director Jonathan Hair
Editor-in-Chief John C. Miles
Picture research Diana Morris

Picture credits
AP/Topham: 16
Bettmann/Corbis: 23
Cody Images: 10, 11, 12, 18, 20, 22bl, 30, 31
HIP/Topham: 15bl
PA/Topham; 28
Picturepoint/Topham: front cover b,
back cover b, 7, 8, 13, 15br, 17, 21, 24, 27, 32
PRO/HIP/Topham: 1, 9
Roger-Viollet/Topham: front cover t,
back cover t, 22br
Topham: 19, 26b

Every attempt has been made to clear copyright.
Should there be any inadvertent omission please apply
to the publisher for rectification.

Dewey classification number: 941.084

ISBN 978 1 4451 4350 7

Printed in China

Franklin Watts
An imprint of
Hachette Children's Group
Part of The Watts Publishing Group
Carmelite House
50 Victoria Embankment
London EC4Y 0DZ

An Hachette UK Company
www.hachette.co.uk

www.franklinwatts.co.uk

Note to parents and teachers:
Every effort has been made by the Publishers
to ensure that the websites in this book
are suitable for children, that they are of
the highest educational value, and that
they contain no inappropriate or offensive
material. However, because of the nature of
the Internet, it is impossible to guarantee that
the contents of these sites will not be altered.
We strongly advise that Internet access is
supervised by a responsible adult.

CONTENTS

A People's War

World War Two (1939-45) is sometimes called "a people's war" because more ordinary people, or civilians, were involved than in any other war before.

Civilian deaths

Civilians had been killed in World War One (1914-18), the first global conflict. But, as these figures show, civilian deaths were far greater in the Second World War and much greater than military deaths.

- **World War One:** 95% of deaths were military, 5% were civilian.
- **World War Two:** 33% of all deaths were military, 67% were civilian.

Records of war

We know a lot about life on the home front. Newsreels, newspapers and photographs give a vivid picture. There are letters from wives, husbands, children and friends who wrote frequently to each other. Wartime diaries also exist. They tell us what it was like to do war work, survive an air raid, take in children or cook with limited rations – all aspects of life on the home front.

The Road to War

During the 1930s, there was a rise of fascism in Europe. The Nazi (National Socialist) Party – an extreme right-wing political party – came to power in Germany under the leadership of Adolf Hitler. In 1938 Nazi Germany invaded Austria and what was then called Czechoslovakia. In 1939 Germany invaded Poland. Britain and its empire, together with France, declared war on Germany and World War Two began. Two years later Germany invaded Russia and Japan bombed America, which also entered the war. World War Two had become global. By its end, the war had involved every continent, and most of the countries of the world.

The Home Front

When war began, many people enlisted to fight. Others remained at home but they were not free from the effects of war. World War Two brought war into people's daily lives in a way that had never happened before in history. For this reason, just as soldiers went to fight on various front lines, civilians were said to be fighting war on the home front, as homes themselves became front lines. The term "home front" was first applied to the British who, in 1940, faced Nazi Germany all on their own. But it can also be applied to civilians in the other warring countries who were caught up in the terrors, dangers and impact of war.

Nazi dictator Adolf Hitler watches as German troops pour into Poland in September 1939, starting World War Two.

Dominance of War

From 1939-45, war dominated everyone's life. Mass bombing brought war to the doorstep as civilians became targets and were killed, wounded or made homeless. Food, clothing and other daily items were rationed or became scarce. Children were separated from their parents, sent away to safety or into labour camps. Industry went on to a war footing and people of all ages worked for the war effort. In some countries, conscription (compulsory call-up) was introduced, bringing whole populations into the labour force or armed services. Those too old to enlist grabbed makeshift weapons and were trained to defend their country or to help with the aftermath of bombing. The lives of virtually everyone in all the warring countries were disrupted by six years of total war.

Timeline of War

1938 German troops march into Czechoslovakia; British government plans for war; gas masks distributed.

Sept 1939 Germany invades Poland; Britain and its empire and France declare war on Germany; British children evacuated to countryside; blackout begins in Britain and Germany; "phoney war" begins.

Jan 1940 Food rationing begins in Britain.

May 1940 Germany invades Low Countries; Local Defence Volunteers (known as the Home Guard) are formed in Britain.

June 1940 German troops enter Paris.

Aug-Sept 1940 Battle of Britain.

Sept 1940 Blitz on British cities begins.

Mar 1941 Conscription (call-up) of British women for war work.

June 1941 Clothes are rationed in Britain; Germany invades Russia.

Nov 1941 Food rationing begins in Russia.

Dec 1941 Japanese bomb Pearl Harbor in Hawaii; USA enters war on Allied side.

Jan 1942 American GIs arrive in Britain; more goods in Britain are rationed.

Feb 1942 Germany rations potatoes.

Mar-Sept 1943 Major Allied bombing offensive against Germany. Fuel and food shortages in all warring countries.

1944 War industry at peak production in the USA, UK and USSR.

June 1944 Allies land in France; German V1 bomb hits Britain.

Aug 1944 Allies liberate Paris.

Feb 1945 Allies devastate Dresden, Germany.

Mar 1945 All Japanese over age of six mobilised for war effort.

7 May 1945 Germany surrenders; 8 May V-E (Victory in Europe) Day.

Aug 1945 Allies drop atomic bombs on Hiroshima and Nagasaki, Japan.

14 Aug 1945 Japan surrenders; World War Two ends.

Being Prepared

As German troops swept through Europe, governments prepared for war. Civilians donned gas masks, dug shelters and switched off lights.

Carrying a gas mask at all times became a way of life for all British citizens.

Hitler will send no warning – so always carry your gas mask

ISSUED BY THE MINISTRY OF HOME SECURITY

The road to war

After the union with Austria in March 1938, Hitler turned his attention to another neighbour, Czechoslovakia. He threatened to invade unless 3 million Germans living in the Sudetenland border region were united with Germany. At a conference in Munich in September, the leaders of Britain, France and Italy agreed to German demands; the Czechs were not consulted. The British Prime Minister Neville Chamberlain said that the Munich agreement provided "peace for our time" but the world was at war only one year later.

Gas Masks

Not everyone in Britain had believed war would happen (see panel, left) but once it did, preparations swung into action. People expected bombing to start at once, with invasion not far behind. Fearing the Germans would use poison gas, the British government distributed 38 million gas masks for civilian use. Smelly and uncomfortable, people had to carry them everywhere. German, US and Japanese civilians also had gas masks. In the event, poison gas was not used.

Shelters, Sandbags and Balloons

Bomb shelters appeared everywhere. The British government gave "Anderson shelters" free to families on low incomes. These were corrugated iron sheets bolted together and placed in the garden. The shelters were covered with soil in which some enterprising families grew vegetables. People piled sandbags against the walls of their homes and put tape on the windows. Some made their own bomb shelters in garages or under the stairs. Bomb shelters were also provided in parks and other public places. Huge, silver barrage balloons were launched. These floated over cities and towns as protection against bombing. A network of steel cables hung below the balloons. Enemy aircraft would have to fly high above the balloons to avoid becoming entangled. In Britain, street names and signposts were taken down to cause confusion in the event of a possible invasion.

Lights Out

In Britain and Germany, a blackout was imposed. No one was allowed to show any light at night, not even by striking a match, in case it attracted enemy bombers. People covered doors and windows with thick curtains. Streetlights were switched off and public buildings were blacked out. Buses and cars had masked headlights and dim blue lights were used in trains. It was an eerie time as people waited for the bombs to arrive.

Striped Cows

At first the blackout caused irritation, accidents and deaths. People stumbled in the dark, and unable to see oncoming cars, died in accidents. After a while, authorities painted white lines on kerbs, steps and lampposts. One farmer painted white stripes on his cows so that people could see them.

Macabre Preparations

Preparations for war were grisly. Authorities expected bombs to cause a high civilian death toll. They made thousands of cardboard coffins and insisted everyone carry an identity card.

"*Put that light out!*"

British air-raid warden's shout

Barrage bolloons with long tethers were used to defend airstrips. Attacking aircraft were prevented from flying low because there was a danger they would become entangled in the tethers extending from the ground to the balloons.

Leaving Home

As war broke out, thousands of British children were sent away from their homes for safety. Later, children in other warring countries were also evacuated.

> ❝ *I like the meadows and parks...
> I miss my home...and I would
> rather be there...I miss my sister
> and my friends...I miss my
> mother's cooking...* ❞

13-year-old girl evacuated to Cambridge

City children were evacuated to the countryside to escape the bombing. Many were billeted with strangers.

Children's transport

From 1938 German Jews were in terrible danger from Nazi persecution. Few countries were prepared to help but the British government reluctantly agreed to take in a certain number of Jewish children aged between 5-17. Between 1938-40, about 10,000 Jewish children left Germany for the safety of Britain. They travelled in sealed trains, which became known as *Kindertransport* (children's transport). Most never saw their parents again: they were murdered in the Holocaust.

Operation Pied Piper

In the first four days of September 1939 about 1.5 million children, pregnant women and disabled people were evacuated from major British cities. It was a massive operation, code-named Operation Pied Piper, after the famous story. Most evacuees were children. They were often organised into groups in school playgrounds and then labelled like parcels. Clutching teddy bears, dolls, a gas mask and a small suitcase, they were marched off in lines to the nearest railway station. From there they were sent to the countryside for safety. Mothers travelled with babies and children under five, but most children went on their own, with the older children taking care of younger ones. None of them knew where they were going or when they would see their parents again.

Staying with Strange Families

Children were billeted (housed) with families they had never met. Some arrived, tired and confused, to find homes had not been arranged for them. They waited in groups while strangers walked around them, deciding which children to take. Most were made welcome and treated kindly. Others had bad experiences of not having enough to eat, being punished and treated like strangers. Some evacuees came from deprived areas. Their host families were shocked to see children with nits, skin diseases and tattered clothing. A few complained that evacuees were badly behaved.

Homesickness

Most evacuees had never left home or the city before. Flowers, fields, even cows, were new. Some found evacuation a big adventure; others were confused and could not cope. Most were homesick. By 1940, when bombing had still not started, some parents began to bring their children home.

Seavacs

Some British children were sent to the USA, Canada, Australia or South Africa. Known as "seavacs", they travelled by ship. In 1940 one ship, the *City of Benares*, carrying 90 seavacs, was torpedoed and sunk. Only 13 children survived.

This poster urges mothers to keep their children living away from cities.

Evacuation timeline

1938-40 About 10,000 Jewish children arrive in Britain via the Kindertransport (a German word meaning children's transport).

1-4 Sept 1939 About 1.5 million people, mainly children, are evacuated from cities and towns in Britain.

January 1940 More than 1 million evacuees return home.

July 1940 Some 213,000 children evacuated from industrial cities in Britain. Children also sent to USA, Canada and Australia.

Sept 17 1940 German torpedo sinks ship *City of Benares*. 77 children aboard killed.

Sept 1940–Dec 1941 More than 1,250,000 British children evacuated.

July 1941 80,000 women and children evacuated from Moscow, USSR; by end of 1942 some 150 factories and 10 million workers had been evacuated from Moscow.

1943 About 1.2 million German children and adults evacuated from bombed cities to the countryside.

June-July 1944 About 1.5 million people leave London to escape flying bombs.

1945 450,000 Japanese children are evacuated from cities to protect them from intensive bombing.

Surviving the Blitz

There was an uneasy calm during the first months of war. The British called it the "phoney war". From 1940, air raids began. Thousands of civilians were killed or made homeless.

A German V-1 flying bomb, or "doodlebug"

Doodlebugs

In 1944, Germany sent new, fearsome weapons against Britain. The first were flying bombs, known as the V1s. V stood for *Vergeltungswaffe* (retaliation weapon). Londoners called them "doodlebugs" because they looked peculiar and made a weird buzzing sound. Civilians knew an explosion was coming because, before the bomb fell, its engine cut out. Doodlebugs killed some 5,000 British civilians. Germany also launched V2s, which were ballistic missiles that arrived without warning.

Blitzing the Cities

Between September 1940 and May 1941 the German *Luftwaffe* (air force) bombed British cities. This was called the Blitz, taken from the German word *Blitzkrieg* (lightning war). London was the main target but Coventry, Glasgow, Birmingham, Hull, Liverpool, Belfast and other British cities were hit as well. From 1942, combined Allied forces pounded German cities such as Hamburg, Berlin and Dresden. Bombing killed civilians in the USSR, Japan, Australia, parts of the USA, Britain and Germany.

Taking Shelter

Night after night wailing sirens warned of incoming raids. Incendiary (fire) bombs rained down; the noise was horrendous. Authorities had not realised what terrible destruction the air raids would bring. Official shelters in Britain and elsewhere were often inadequate so people looked for alternatives. Many Londoners made for the Underground, thousands sleeping on platforms or, after the power was switched off, stringing hammocks between the rails. Elsewhere, people huddled in Anderson shelters, or stayed in their homes or in makeshift shelters until the "all clear" siren sounded. Civilians in Moscow sheltered in the Metro when Germany bombed the USSR in 1941. In Japan some civilians dug pitiful shelters in their back gardens during mass bombing raids in 1944-45.

A British woman air-raid warden rescues a child from a bombed-out house after an air raid.

Bombing statistics:

Britain and Germany 1940-45

• **Britain:** 60,400 civilians killed; 85,000 seriously injured; 2 million homes destroyed. More than one in ten air-raid victims were children.

• **Germany:** 600,000 civilians killed; 800,000 seriously injured; 3.37 million homes destroyed. Children made up one-fifth of the dead.

Aftermath

When people emerged from shelters they saw fires and rubble. As fire fighters brought fires under control, air-raid wardens saved trapped people. Volunteers such as the WVS (Women's Voluntary Service) in Britain provided shocked civilians with blankets, tea and assistance. Thousands were made homeless. Living with nightly bombing became part of life. People tried to carry on as normal, going to work after raids even if offices and shops had been bombed.

Dresden firestorm

In 1945 Allied forces bombed the German city of Dresden. More than 700 British Lancaster bombers and 500 American bombers hit the city in an attack that caused what became known as a firestorm. Planes dropped clusters of incendiary bombs filled with combustible chemicals. As the targeted areas caught fire the air became hot and rose. Cold air rushed in at ground level, sucking people into the firestorm. The city was destroyed and more than 135,000 people died. Even at the time the attack was condemned.

Food Rationing

Food rationing was part of daily life on every home front. People in the USSR and German-occupied territories suffered particularly terrible hardships.

British Restaurants

The British government set up communal eating places, known as British Restaurants. They served cheap, healthy meals using non-rationed foods. One dish – Woolton Pie, named after Lord Woolton, minister for food – consisted of parsnips, potatoes and carrots, topped with oatmeal. It became a wartime joke.

Healthy diets

The British wartime diet was basic but healthy. Every child was given orange juice, cod liver oil and a daily pint of milk. The oil tasted horribly fishy but was rich in vitamins. There had been a worldwide economic depression during the 1930s. Wartime rations meant some poorer people ate better during the war than before it.

Rationing Begins

In 1940 Britain rationed butter, ham, bacon, tea, meat, eggs, cheese and sugar. Fresh fruit was scarce; imported fruits like bananas disappeared. Families had ration books and registered with their grocer and butcher. Prices were fixed and shopkeepers marked ration books when families bought food. Germany had a similar scheme using colour-coded books.

Being Inventive

As shortages increased, people spent hours queueing for food but items were often simply not available. The British government bombarded families with recipes. Root vegetables were not rationed, so cartoon characters like "Potato Pete" and "Doctor Carrot" encouraged housewives to cook with them. Women used carrots to sweeten puddings and used potatoes in every way imaginable. There were even recipes for carrot "fudge" and "marmalade".

Substitute Foods

People learnt to cook unusual foods like pigs' brains, liver or cows' udders instead of beef and lamb. Whale meat replaced fish, but was never popular. Dried milk and eggs were used. Mixed with water, dried eggs produced rubbery omelettes. Soya and lentils made meatless sausages. Margarine replaced butter and Spam, tinned chopped pork from the USA, became popular. In Germany, ground acorns replaced fresh coffee to make a foul-tasting drink.

"Dig for Victory!"

The British government urged people to "dig for victory" by growing their own food. Lawns and flowerbeds were turned into vegetable allotments. People kept pigs, chickens and rabbits to add to their rations. They picked and bottled home-grown fruits like apples and pears, or gathered berries. It was an offence to waste anything.

Starvation

Despite shortages, people in Britain had enough to eat. In Germany, food shortages became severe by 1943. In occupied France people had to cook nettles and other wild plants. In Holland people ate tulip bulbs, and some 16,000 people starved to death. In the USSR thousands died of hunger.

A wartime gardener shows children how to use garden tools in an allotment.

Weekly rations

This was the average weekly wartime food ration for one British adult:

Bacon or ham	4 oz (115 g)
Meat	To the value of 1s 2d (about 6p today)
Butter	2 oz (56 g)
Cheese	2 oz (56 g). Sometimes more depending on availability
Margarine	4 oz (115 g)
Cooking fat	4 oz (115g) but often less
Milk	3 pints (1.7 litres), often less
Dried milk	1 packet (4 pints/2.3 litres) every 4 weeks
Sugar	8 oz (225 g)
Jams	1 lb (500 g) every 2 months
Tea	2 oz (56g)
Eggs	1 but often less
Dried eggs	1 packet of 12 dried eggs every 4 weeks
Sweets	3 oz (87 g)

A full week's British wartime food ration.

Utility Fashions

As war continued, clothes were rationed and all sorts of daily items disappeared or became scarce. People saved, mended and recycled everything.

No Frills

People in wartime could not buy clothes whenever they wanted to because items were on ration. From 1941, in Britain, people could only buy clothes worth a certain number of points each year. A man's coat was 16 points; a pair of shoes was 5 points. In 1941 the allowance was 60 points; by 1944 it had dropped to 20.

To save material, manufacturers made plain, simple clothes, following strict government rules. They were known as "Utility" clothes. Jackets were plain, with boxed shoulders. Skirts were short, worn above the knee, and straight. There were no zips as metal was needed for weapons. Even in the USA, where shortages were far less severe, people adopted wartime fashions. Working women wore trousers or dungarees, headscarves and flat-soled shoes.

Women's wartime fashion had fewer frills, but remained stylish.

Half-size stamps

Paper was scarce so wartime newspapers were thin, often with the wood-pulp chips showing through. In South Africa, postage stamps were printed half their usual size to save paper.

Making Do

People on the home front made do with what they had. Instead of buying new clothes, people mended old ones to make them last. Cast-off adult clothes were turned into children's clothes. Women made clothes out of bedspreads, sheets, curtains, blankets and parachute silk. Nylon stockings disappeared as nylon was needed for parachutes, so women dyed their legs with shoe polish or gravy browning, and drew stocking seams up the back of their legs using an eyebrow pencil.

Shortages

Basic goods became scarce, including leather, rubber, soap, toilet paper, even knicker elastic. When leather was scarce, shoes were made with wooden soles. Wartime soap was grey in colour. Water and coal were restricted. Having a bath was a chilly business as no one was supposed to use more than 12 cm of water. Petrol was rationed because it was needed for military vehicles. In France and Australia, some people used charcoal-burning attachments on their cars but almost everywhere people walked or cycled.

Got any Gum?

North America had rationing but did not endure the same shortages as Britain did. American GIs who were posted to Britain from 1942 to 1945 were shocked by the grey drabness. They brought scented soap, nylon stockings, cigarettes, chocolates and chewing gum with them, luxuries the British rarely saw. British children trailed after American soldiers, asking: "Got any gum, chum?"

" Knitted goods were unravelled and re-knit, holes were embroidered over. Growing girls had multicoloured dresses because two were made into one.… No hair clips or curlers, no safety pins, no matches, no leather-soled shoes. "

BBC People's War: Bradford Archives

Women hand-knitted their jumpers during the war years.

Doing Your Bit

Everyone on the home front was urged to "do their bit" for the war effort. Civilians responded in every way they could.

War bonds

In the USA, men, women and children helped to fund the costs of war by buying Victory bonds. Children spent pocket money on war stamps, which cost only a few cents. They glued them into a book and exchanged these for war bonds. In all, American families raised about $135 billion.

Volunteering Help

When war broke out, men of suitable age were called up for the armed forces and went to fight. Some were not called up immediately because they were in "reserved" occupations such as engineering and were needed for war work. Other civilians volunteered to help in many ways. They worked as air raid wardens, making sure the blackout was maintained and helping people into shelters. They stood watch at night, searching the skies for enemy aircraft. Some staffed anti-aircraft guns or helped to launch and navigate huge barrage balloons.

Older women joined organisations like the WVS, helping bombed-out civilians, running canteens for soldiers, giving out clothes to the needy and assisting refugees. Civilians everywhere worked as fire fighters, drivers, nurses, special constables and first-aid workers. They knitted clothes for soldiers, took in evacuees, collected scrap and did whatever they could for the war effort.

Home Guard

Some civilians organised to defend their country. In Britain, the Local Defence Volunteers (Home Guard) was set up, with nearly a million men. It was nicknamed "Dad's Army" since some of the men in it were too old to fight. Its job was to protect civilians if Germans invaded. Although poorly equipped, the Home Guard drilled and practised enthusiastically. Germany did not invade and it disbanded in 1944.

Women worked hard on the land and in factories. Here, two munitions workers assemble shells.

War Work

Industries switched from peacetime production to manufacturing weapons, tanks, ships, aircraft, parachutes and other necessities of war. Some skilled male workers remained on the home front but, as increasing numbers were called up, women replaced them. In Britain, Canada, the USA and the USSR, thousands of women entered the workforce, some for the first time and many doing work previously only performed by men.

Women worked in munitions factories, shipyards and aircraft production; they trained as carpenters, painters and welders. The hours were long and conditions were dirty and dangerous, particularly in munitions factories. Wartime production soared, mostly due to women's work. Civilians who had never farmed before worked on the land to boost food supplies. On the home front everyone was brought in to the war effort. In Britain, Italian and German prisoners of war (POWs) were put to work on the land.

❝ Life was absolutely consumed by the war. And if people forgot, there was always someone around to remind them by repeating the common saying 'Don't you know there's a war on?' ❞

Dot Chastney, American schoolgirl

Scrap for Spitfires

In 1940 the British government appealed to civilians to collect scrap for aircraft production. People pulled up metal railings and handed in mountains of metal household goods, such as frying pans, coat hangers, tin baths and teapots, to be melted down. Much of the scrap was not used but people watched Spitfires overhead, wondering if their frying pan had helped to make them. American, Japanese, Russian and German civilians also collected scrap for weapons.

Children and War

War affected children just as much as adults. Though parents tried to protect them, children experienced air raids, rationing, terror and danger. Many died or were orphaned.

Two girls at the seaside stare through a tangle of barbed wire intended to slow down an invasion.

> **The most scary time was when the Germans were sending over the doodlebugs. ... all you could do was wait and hope it missed you ...**
>
> *Derek White, British civilian*

Trauma and death

Children lived with the fear of death. They spent sleepless nights in shelters, terrified by sounds and sights. Many were made homeless or orphaned. They lost parents, brothers, sisters and friends. Some were buried alive in rubble and had to wait hours to be rescued. Evacuated children worried about their parents' safety. Children in the Channel Islands and mainland Europe experienced the confusion of invasion. Jewish children suffered dreadfully. In Germany, Poland, Hungary and other occupied countries thousands were rounded up and sent to their deaths in labour and concentration camps.

Disrupted Schooling

Parents and teachers tried hard to keep life normal for children but their studies suffered. They went to school but lessons were often disrupted by bombings and evacuations, especially in cities. Makeshift schools were set up but paper, books and teachers were in short supply. When sirens sounded lessons stopped, sometimes for hours. Children played truant, staying away for weeks or not going to school at all. Some helped at home, looking after younger children while mothers were at work. By 1945, half of Britain's children had difficulty reading and writing.

Doing their Bit

Children did their bit for the war effort. In all the warring countries, they collected scrap metal, tin foil, paper and glass for recycling. Older children ran messages during air raids, helped to clear rubble and gave first aid. Schoolchildren "adopted" soldiers, ships or submarines. They knitted clothes and sent food parcels and letters. They raised money by buying war stamps or holding fund-raising events. Most British people aged 14-17 were in full-time war work. In Japan, Germany and the Soviet Union, much younger children were enlisted into the workforce making gun parts or rainproof clothes for the armed forces. In the USA, from 1942, millions of young people aged 12-17 joined the workforce for the duration of the war.

Fun, Games and Comics

Despite war, children managed to have fun. For some, war itself was exciting. Children plotted its progress on wall maps using little paper flags. In 1940 British children watched the Battle of Britain taking place overhead. Many remember being enthralled and excited. Children played on bombsites, acting out dogfights and collecting pieces of shrapnel. It could be dangerous: some children died from disturbing unexploded bombs.

Children in Nazi Germany

In Germany, all non-Jewish girls and boys had to join Nazi youth organisations. Boys joined the Hitler Youth. Girls joined the League of German Girls.

Boys and girls drilled and wore uniforms. They were taught to love the Fatherland and to obey without question. As the tide of war turned against Germany, young boys were recruited to fight.

Fun didn't stop during the war. Here, six young evacuees run along a country road, each carrying a box with his gas mask inside.

This is the News

People on the home front listened to the wireless (radio) daily. It was a lifeline for them, providing news, boosting morale and spreading propaganda.

Spy mania

Rumours about spies or Germans disguised as nuns being parachuted into the country swept through Britain in 1940. Government poster campaigns urged civilians to be careful about talking in public. Slogans such as "Careless Talk Costs Lives" or "Walls have Ears" appeared on posters everywhere. Spy mania reached horrendous proportions. In Britain, residents of German origin and refugees were rounded up and interned (detained) on the Isle of Man. In 1942 more than 119,000 Japanese-Americans living on the West Coast of the USA were placed in detention camps.

You never know who's listening!

CARELESS TALK COSTS LIVES

News Broadcasts

Most people heard the announcement of war on their radio. The BBC (British Broadcasting Corporation) issued regular news bulletins throughout the war and kept the home front informed. Vivid eyewitness accounts of aerial battles were broadcast. Pre-recorded news events and interviews with evacuated children or troops serving on the front line were later broadcast to families at home.

By 1945, the BBC was broadcasting news in more than 40 languages, sending radio programmes to people in Nazi-occupied countries as well as Britain. While British families listened to the radio in their sitting rooms, those in occupied countries listened in

Listening to the wireless was both popular and necessary.

secret, risking death just for owning a radio. As the Allies advanced, even families in Nazi Germany tuned in to the BBC for news.

❝I used to listen to the radio avidly…that was our only means of communication. There was no television.❞

Doris Scott, British civilian

Boosting Morale

Radio boosted civilian morale and encouraged patriotism (love of one's country). In Japan and Germany, radios broadcast marching tunes and urged people to make greater efforts. In 1941, Soviet leader Joseph Stalin spoke on radio to the Russian people, urging them to resist the Germans using what he called a "scorched-earth policy". British Prime Minister Winston Churchill broadcast stirring messages of hope and encouragement to the home front that many people still remember today. US President Roosevelt gave regular broadcasts and exiled leaders, such as the Dutch royal family, used radio to send positive messages to their people. Resistance leaders, such as Frenchman General Charles de Gaulle, sent coded messages through the BBC to underground fighters in occupied territories.

Misinformation

Both sides also used radio to undermine morale on the home front. An English Nazi sympathiser, William Joyce, made broadcasts from Berlin to Britain giving misleading information about the war. US-born Japanese Iva Ikuko Toguri, called "Tokyo Rose", broadcast stories intended to destroy morale to US forces in the Pacific.

Propaganda images

Newspapers, hoardings, posters and magazines were all used to spread government propaganda. Recruitment posters urged civilians to join the army, work on the land or go to work in the factories. Many used graphic images or presented the enemy in cartoon form. In Nazi Germany, posters were used to portray Jews as monsters.

Iva Ikuko Toguri - also known as "Tokyo Rose" - behind bars.

Having Fun

Despite the war, civilians found time to enjoy themselves. They listened to music, laughed at radio comedy, danced, sang and went to the cinema.

Dancing at the Savoy

The Savoy Hotel in London was very grand. During air raids as many as 300 guests danced and dined in their luxurious air-raid shelter. Hotel staff handed out mattresses and pillows and guests slept on the basement floor in full evening dress.

Socialising in shelters

During the Blitz, British civilians spent so much time in air-raid shelters that they organised entertainment for themselves. In one large London underground shelter, a committee planned weekly activities. These included community singing, darts and keep-fit classes. Someone even brought a piano into the shelter.

Music and Comedy

The radio provided entertainment as well as news. In Britain, there were programmes like *Music While You Work* for workers on the home front, and shows for the armed forces, which civilians also tuned into. One, called *Sincerely Yours*, featured Vera Lynn, nicknamed the "Forces Sweetheart". Her sentimental song "We'll Meet Again" became a wartime classic.

Comedy programmes were popular. In Britain, the best known was *ITMA* (*It's That Man Again*). Featuring the comedian Tommy Handley, it mixed slapstick and satire and its catchphrases became part of daily language. Thousands tuned in every week.

Cinema and theatre-going was popular during the war, as this scene shows.

Dancing the Night Away

Big dance bands attracted huge audiences. Dances were held in village halls, converted fire stations and in big city ballrooms. Young women and men, often soldiers stationed a long way from home, went dancing whenever they could because no one knew what the next day would bring. Young British women did the waltz, rumba and jitterbug with American, Polish and Commonwealth soldiers, all of whom were stationed in Britain. People also danced at home to popular music on the radio or on scratchy 78 rpm records played on gramophones (record players). Classical music was popular too. The London Promenade Concerts (known as the "Proms") continued throughout the war and were always well attended.

Going to the Cinema

People flocked to the cinema every week. British cinemas had closed in 1939 for fear of air raids but they soon reopened. Managers posted notices advising people to leave the cinema when air-raid sirens sounded but hardly anyone did. Films gave people a chance to forget about the war. For just a few pence, they could see a movie, newsreel, an information film and a full-length feature film. Filmmakers in Hollywood and Britain produced Westerns, patriotic films, romances and cartoons throughout the war. *Gone with the Wind*, starring Clarke Gable and Vivien Leigh, was a massive hit: it ran continuously in London's West End during the war. Another was *Casablanca,* starring Ingrid Bergman and Humphrey Bogart.

Wartime hits

Popular music flourished. There were sentimental hits, catchy patriotic songs and jazzy tunes. Played on radios, gramophones and in dance halls, they were sung and hummed by everyone. Favourite wartime hits included:

A Nightingale Sang in Berkeley Square Vera Lynn
As Time Goes By Dooley Wilson (from *Casablanca*)
Boogie Woogie Bugle Boy Andrews Sisters
Don't Get Around Much Anymore Duke Ellington
Elmer's Tune Glenn Miller
I'll Be With You in Apple Blossom Time Andrews Sisters
I'll Never Smile Again Frank Sinatra
In the Mood Glen Miller
Is You Is Or Is You Ain't My Baby Louis Jordan
Moonlight Becomes You Bing Crosby
White Christmas Bing Crosby
Roll Out the Barrel
Sentimental Journey Les Brown Orchestra
Take the 'A' Train Duke Ellington
We'll Meet Again Vera Lynn
We're Gonna Hang Out the Washing on the Siegfried Line
When the Lights Go On Again All Over the World Vaughn Monroe
You Always Hurt the One You Love Sammy Kaye

Love and Marriage

With the future uncertain, couples rushed into marriage. Weddings were hasty and couples were often separated shortly after marrying.

Wartime weddings

People married in churches, air-raid shelters or military bases. Brides borrowed wedding dresses or made them from parachute silk and muslin. Cake ingredients were scarce. Women used white rice paper to look like icing or put a decorated cardboard covering over a wartime sponge cake.

Wedding and Separation

Marriage boomed when the war broke out. Many couples married quickly, fearing they might not survive the war. The number of weddings began to drop but war threw people together in unexpected ways. In the heightened emotions of the time, people looking for romance met and fell in love.

Within hours of getting married, new husbands were posted abroad. They might return home briefly on leave but couples were often separated for months or years at a time. Wives worried about their husbands' safety. Often the only news they received was to learn that their husband had been killed or taken prisoner. Wives on the home front were anxious and lonely.

Changing Patterns

War changed behaviour. Before the war, teenage girls had very restricted lives. Now most worked for the war effort. Many lived away from home and made the most of their new freedom, going to dances, parties and meeting servicemen. Some teenagers and young women had brief love affairs.

New Friends

By 1944 there were nearly 1.5 million Allied soldiers stationed in Britain. Most were North American. To the British, American GIs, with their smart uniforms, good pay and easy manners were "like Hollywood come to life". Not surprisingly, young British women were bowled over by them. At the end of the war, about 80,000 British women went to the USA as brides and 41,000 went to Canada, to take up new lives as married women there.

Single Mothers

Thousands of men were killed in action leaving widowed mothers to bring up children alone. In Britain, more than 300,000 children were born to single women, often as a result of a brief affair. At that time it was difficult to be an unmarried mother. Many were criticised for "improper" behaviour, there was no government assistance and they had to give up war work when they became pregnant. Some went into homes for unmarried mothers. Most put their babies up for adoption. Only a few women dared to keep their babies.

British women who have married American soldiers board a ship after the war to go to the USA and join their husbands.

Blue and gold stars

American women put blue stars on white banners and hung them out of the window to show how many family members (sons, husbands, brothers) were fighting in the armed forces. When someone in the family was killed in action, women replaced a blue star with a gold one. As war continued, the gold stars increased.

> **"There is no doubt that Jack was killed... Today, I have been so heartbroken. I cannot believe that I shall never see Jack again..."**
>
> *Louise White, British civilian, on the death of her husband, an RAF gunner*

Wartime Christmas

Christmas was difficult. Families were separated with many fathers and husbands killed, away fighting or imprisoned. Presents were scarce. Mothers made new toys or spruced up old ones. They decorated trees with coloured buttons and saved ration coupons so children would wake on Christmas morning to chocolate and sweets in their stockings.

Lights on Again

World War Two ended in 1945. After six years of war, blackouts ended and the lights came on again. Civilians celebrated but the losses had been enormous.

Rejoicing on Wall Street in New York as the war in Europe ends, 8 May 1945.

World War Two: Civilian deaths

Figures for civilian deaths vary but these give an approximate picture. Greatest losses occurred in countries where civilians were bombed, invaded or both.

USSR	17 million
Poland	5.86 million
Yugoslavia	1.35 million
Germany	2.44 million
Hungary	600,000
Romania	465,000
France	350,000
Japan	350,000
Czechoslovakia	315,000
Holland	236,000
Italy	153,000
Greece	140,000
Great Britain	92,700
Bulgaria	50,000
Belgium	23,000
USA	6,000

Celebrations

War in Europe ended in May 1945. In Britain, the BBC announced the end of fighting in Europe. Streetlights were switched on for the first time in six years, people tore down their blackout curtains and organised street parties, bonfires and victory parades. Children were given rare treats: fruit, sweets and ice cream. Millions celebrated in London, Paris and Moscow as well as towns, villages and cities throughout the Allied countries. Three months later, in August 1945, Japan surrendered, ending the war in Asia. In the USA, more than a million people filled Times Square in New York City to celebrate.

> **"I do remember having oranges for the first time, at the VE parties. I ate the peel and I was sick because I didn't realise that was a thing you didn't do."**
>
> *Peter Bennett, British civilian*

Devastation

Six years of war had caused dreadful devastation in Britain, the USSR, Germany, Japan and much of mainland Europe. In Germany, Italy and Japan, defeated civilians wandered through the rubble of their homes, starving and disorientated. Millions of civilians had lost their lives worldwide and major cities and towns all bore the scars of war.

Difficulties

Peace did not mean an instant return to normality. In Britain rationing continued until 1954; there were food and fuel shortages. Even bread was rationed, which had not happened during the war. Thousands of families were homeless and cities littered with bombsites. Children who had spent the war in the USA or Canada were reunited with their families but after the comforts they had known many were shocked by Britain's austerity. As servicemen came home, wives and children had to get to know husbands and fathers who seemed like strangers. Orphaned children and bereaved wives suffered emotional scars that lasted for years.

Atomic devastation

On 6 August 1945, a US B-29 aircraft dropped an atomic bomb on the Japanese city of Hiroshima to try to force the Japanese to surrender and end the war. The city was flattened and about 200,000 people died outright. Three days later a second atomic bomb was dropped on Nagasaki. About 141,000 civilians were killed and some 51,000 buildings destroyed. Thousands more died later from dreadful injuries and radiation sickness.

People are still dying today from the long-term effects of radiation. Every year, on 6 August, people in Hiroshima and around the world mark Hiroshima Day with peace vigils and marches. Some launch little paper boats carrying candles onto water to remember the dead.

Rebuilding and welfare

Slowly conditions began to improve. War had boosted the American economy and US aid helped to rebuild much of Europe. In Britain, reforms were brought in that had been planned during the war. The National Health Service was set up to provide free healthcare and dentistry. Mass education opened up learning. By the 1960s, most economies were booming once again.

Glossary

Allies Britain and its empire, France, USA, USSR and others who fought together against Nazi Germany. Germany, Italy and Japan were known as the Axis powers.

Anderson shelter A type of bomb shelter. Made of corrugated iron, and put into a garden, it was named after the British Home Secretary, Sir John Anderson.

Axis powers Germany, Italy, Japan, and other countries that fought against Britain and the Allies.

Billet Temporary housing or other accommodation given to soldiers or evacuees.

Blackout Switching off all lights at night so enemy aircraft would not be able to see houses or factories.

Dogfight Aerial battle between fighter planes.

Evacuation Movement of people from dangerous places to safety.

Fascism Extreme right-wing nationalist movement that began in Italy in 1922. The fascists glorified their leader, to whom they gave total obedience. They believed that the state should have absolute power and that pride in the nation was essential. The term fascist is sometimes used to describe any extreme right-wing movement, including Hitler's National Socialist (Nazi) Party.

GI Nickname for an American soldier. GI stands for Government Issue. American soldiers received GI trousers, GI shirts and other GI items and eventually took the nickname "GI".

Holocaust The term given to the mass murder of Jews by the Nazis in World War Two.

Intern To force people, usually prisoners or foreigners, to live in a particular place such as an internment camp.

Nazi National Socialist. The extreme right-wing political party that came to power in Germany under the leadership of Adolf Hitler.

"Phoney war" Name given to the period of apparent calm after war was declared in September 1939 and April 1940, when Germany invaded Norway.

Pied Piper According to legend, a mysterious stranger wearing multi-coloured clothes and playing a pipe led children out of the medieval town of Hamelin in Germany. The British government used the term "Pied Piper" for the mass evacuation of children from cities in 1939.

Propaganda Information put out in radio broadcasts, leaflets and posters by governments to influence what people do.

Rationing A fixed allowance of food, provisions, fuel and so on set by the government especially in times of scarcity, such as war.

Root vegetables Any plant that has an edible root, such as carrots, turnips, swedes, parsnips and potatoes.

Scorched-earth policy The burning of crops and removal or destruction of anything else that might be useful to an enemy.

Shrapnel Shell, bomb or bullet fragments.

Spam Supply Pressed American Meat, Spam for short. Tinned meat product, mainly made from ham.

Spitfire British fighter aeroplane.

Sudetenland Mountainous region in northern Bohemia, now part of the Czech Republic. Nazi Germany took over the region in 1938.

USSR The world's first communist state. It existed from 1917-91 and included what is now called Russia. It was also known as the Soviet Union.

WEBSITES

http://home.freeuk.net/elloughton13/wwar.htm

www.nationalarchives.gov.uk/education/homefront/

www.bbc.co.uk/history/home_front

www.iwm.org.uk/learning/resources/the-1940s-house www.historyplace.com/worldwar2/timeline/ww2time.htm

www.bbc.co.uk/history/ww2peopleswar/
    An archive of memories of the war, collected by the BBC.

www.bbc.co.uk/schools/primaryhistory/world_war2/

Index